Key Facts on Russia

Essential Information on Russia
By Patrick W. Nee

The Internationalist®
www.internationalist.com

The Internationalist®

International Business, Investment, and Travel

Published by:

The Internationalist Publishing Company

96 Walter Street/ Suite 200

Boston, MA 02131, USA

Tel: 617-354-7722

www.internationalist.com

PN@internationalist.com

Table of Contents

Chapter 1: Background:

Founded in the 12th century, the Principality of Muscovy, was able to emerge from over 200 years of Mongol domination (13th-15th centuries) and to gradually conquer and absorb surrounding principalities. In the early 17th century, a new Romanov Dynasty continued this policy of expansion across Siberia to the Pacific. Under PETER I (ruled 1682-1725), hegemony was extended to the Baltic Sea and the country was renamed the Russian Empire. During the 19th century, more territorial acquisitions were made in Europe and Asia. Defeat in the Russo-Japanese War of 1904-05 contributed to the Revolution of 1905, which resulted in the formation of a parliament and other reforms. Repeated devastating defeats of the Russian army in World War I led to widespread rioting in the major cities of the Russian Empire and to the overthrow in 1917 of the imperial household. The Communists under Vladimir LENIN seized power soon after and formed the USSR. The brutal rule of Iosif STALIN (1928-53) strengthened Communist rule and Russian dominance of the Soviet Union at a cost of tens of millions of lives. The Soviet economy and society stagnated in the following decades until General Secretary Mikhail GORBACHEV (1985-91) introduced glasnost (openness) and perestroika (restructuring) in an attempt to modernize Communism, but his initiatives inadvertently released forces that by December 1991 splintered the USSR into Russia and 14 other independent republics. Since then, Russia has shifted its post-Soviet democratic ambitions in favor of a centralized semi-authoritarian state in which the leadership seeks to legitimize its rule through managed national elections, populist appeals by President PUTIN, and continued economic growth. Russia has severely disabled a Chechen rebel movement, although violence still occurs throughout the North Caucasus.

Chapter 2: Geography

Location:
North Asia bordering the Arctic Ocean, extending from Europe (the portion west of the Urals) to the North Pacific Ocean

Geographic coordinates:
60 00 N, 100 00 E

Map references:
Asia

Area:
total: 17,098,242 sq km
country comparison to the world: 1
land: 16,377,742 sq km
water: 720,500 sq km

Area - comparative:
approximately 1.8 times the size of the US

Land boundaries:
total: 20,241.5 km
border countries: Azerbaijan 284 km, Belarus 959 km, China (southeast) 3,605 km, China (south) 40 km, Estonia 290 km, Finland 1,313 km, Georgia 723 km, Kazakhstan 6,846 km, North Korea 17.5 km, Latvia 292 km, Lithuania (Kaliningrad Oblast) 227 km, Mongolia 3,441 km, Norway 196 km, Poland (Kaliningrad Oblast) 432 km, Ukraine 1,576 km

Coastline:
37,653 km

Maritime claims:
territorial sea: 12 nm
contiguous zone: 24 nm
exclusive economic zone: 200 nm
continental shelf: 200 m depth or to the depth of exploitation

Climate:

ranges from steppes in the south through humid
continental in much of European Russia; subarctic in
Siberia to tundra climate in the polar north; winters
vary from cool along Black Sea coast to frigid in
Siberia; summers vary from warm in the steppes to
cool along Arctic coast

Terrain:

broad plain with low hills west of Urals; vast
coniferous forest and tundra in Siberia; uplands and
mountains along southern border regions

Elevation extremes:

lowest point: Caspian Sea -28 m

highest point: Gora El'brus 5,633 m (highest point in
Europe)

Natural resources:

wide natural resource base including major deposits of
oil, natural gas, coal, and many strategic minerals,
reserves of rare earth elements, timber

note: formidable obstacles of climate, terrain, and
distance hinder exploitation of natural resources

Land use:

arable land: 7.17%

permanent crops: 0.11%

other: 92.72% (2005)

Irrigated land:

43,460 sq km (2003)

Total renewable water resources:

4,498 cu km (1997)

Freshwater withdrawal (domestic/industrial/agricultural):

total: 76.68 cu km/yr (19%/63%/18%)

per capita: 535 cu m/yr (2000)

Natural hazards:

permafrost over much of Siberia is a major
impediment to development; volcanic activity in the
Kuril Islands; volcanoes and earthquakes on the
Kamchatka Peninsula; spring floods and

summer/autumn forest fires throughout Siberia and parts of European Russia

volcanism: significant volcanic activity on the Kamchatka Peninsula and Kuril Islands; the peninsula alone is home to some 29 historically active volcanoes, with dozens more in the Kuril Islands; Kliuchevskoi (elev. 4,835 m), which erupted in 2007 and 2010, is Kamchatka's most active volcano; Avachinsky and Koryaksky volcanoes, which pose a threat to the city of Petropavlovsk-Kamchatskiy, have been deemed "Decade Volcanoes" by the International Association of Volcanology and Chemistry of the Earth's Interior, worthy of study due to their explosive history and close proximity to human populations; other notable historically active volcanoes include Bezymianny, Chikurachki, Ebeko, Gorely, Grozny, Karymsky, Ketoi, Kronotsky, Ksudach, Medvezhia, Mutnovsky, Sarychev Peak, Shiveluch, Tiatia, Tolbachik, and Zheltovsky

Environment - current issues:

air pollution from heavy industry, emissions of coal-fired electric plants, and transportation in major cities; industrial, municipal, and agricultural pollution of inland waterways and seacoasts; deforestation; soil erosion; soil contamination from improper application of agricultural chemicals; scattered areas of sometimes intense radioactive contamination; groundwater contamination from toxic waste; urban solid waste management; abandoned stocks of obsolete pesticides

Environment - international agreements:

party to: Air Pollution, Air Pollution-Nitrogen Oxides, Air Pollution-Sulfur 85, Antarctic-Environmental Protocol, Antarctic-Marine Living Resources, Antarctic Seals, Antarctic Treaty, Biodiversity, Climate Change, Climate Change-Kyoto Protocol, Desertification, Endangered Species, Environmental Modification, Hazardous Wastes, Law of the Sea,

Marine Dumping, Ozone Layer Protection, Ship
Pollution, Tropical Timber 83, Wetlands, Whaling
<u>signed, but not ratified</u>: Air Pollution-Sulfur 94

Geography - note:

largest country in the world in terms of area but
unfavorably located in relation to major sea lanes of
the world; despite its size, much of the country lacks
proper soils and climates (either too cold or too dry)
for agriculture; Mount El'brus is Europe's tallest peak;
Lake Baikal, the deepest lake in the world, is
estimated to hold one fifth of the world's fresh water

Chapter 3: People and Society

Nationality:

    noun: Russian(s)

    adjective: Russian

Ethnic groups:

    Russian 79.8%, Tatar 3.8%, Ukrainian 2%, Bashkir 1.2%, Chuvash 1.1%, other or unspecified 12.1% (2002 census)

Languages:

    Russian (official), many minority languages

Religions:

    Russian Orthodox 15-20%, Muslim 10-15%, other Christian 2% (2006 est.)

    note: estimates are of practicing worshipers; Russia has large populations of non-practicing believers and non-believers, a legacy of over seven decades of Soviet rule

Population:

    142,517,670 (July 2012 est.)

    country comparison to the world: 9

Age structure:

    0-14 years: 15.7% (male 11,498,268/female 10,890,853)

    15-24 years: 12.4% (male 9,031,057/female 8,662,557)

    25-54 years: 45.8% (male 31,894,116/female 33,432,996)

    55-64 years: 13.1% (male 7,926,184/female 10,711,347)

    65 years and over: 13% (male 5,622,464/female 12,847,828) (2012 est.)

Median age:

    total: 38.8 years

    male: 35.6 years

    female: 42.1 years (2012 est.)

Population growth rate:

    -0.01% (2012 est.)

    country comparison to the world: 192

Birth rate:

    12.3 births/1,000 population (2012 est.)

    country comparison to the world: 160

Death rate:

14.1 deaths/1,000 population (July 2012 est.)

country comparison to the world: 11

Net migration rate:

0.29 migrant(s)/1,000 population (2012 est.)

country comparison to the world: 68

Urbanization:

urban population: 73% of total population (2010)

rate of urbanization: -0.2% annual rate of change (2010-15 est.)

Major cities - population:

MOSCOW (capital) 10.523 million; Saint Petersburg 4.575 million; Novosibirsk 1.397 million; Yekaterinburg 1.344 million; Nizhniy Novgorod 1.267 million (2009)

Sex ratio:

at birth: 1.06 male(s)/female

under 15 years: 1.06 male(s)/female

15-64 years: 0.91 male(s)/female

65 years and over: 0.43 male(s)/female

total population: 0.85 male(s)/female (2011 est.)

Maternal mortality rate:

34 deaths/100,000 live births (2010)

country comparison to the world: 120

Infant mortality rate:

total: 7.3 deaths/1,000 live births

country comparison to the world: 160

male: 8.2 deaths/1,000 live births

female: 6.4 deaths/1,000 live births (2012 est.)

Life expectancy at birth:

total population: 66.46 years

country comparison to the world: 164

male: 60.11 years

female: 73.18 years (2012 est.)

Total fertility rate:

1.61 children born/woman (2012 est.)

country comparison to the world: 178

Health expenditures:

5.4% of GDP (2009)

country comparison to the world: 132

Physicians density:

4.309 physicians/1,000 population (2006)

Hospital bed density:

9.66 beds/1,000 population (2006)

Sanitation facility access:

improved:

urban: 93% of population

rural: 70% of population

total: 87% of population

unimproved:

urban: 7% of population

rural: 30% of population

total: 13% of population

HIV/AIDS - adult prevalence rate:

1% (2009 est.)

country comparison to the world: 46

HIV/AIDS - people living with HIV/AIDS:

980,000 (2009 est.)

country comparison to the world: 10

Major infectious diseases:

degree of risk: intermediate

food or waterborne diseases: bacterial diarrhea

vectorborne disease: tickborne encephalitis

note: highly pathogenic H5N1 avian influenza has been identified in this country; it poses a negligible risk with extremely rare cases possible among US citizens who have close contact with birds (2009)

Education expenditures:

3.9% of GDP (2006)

country comparison to the world: 107

Literacy:

definition: age 15 and over can read and write

total population: 99.6%

male: 99.7%

female: 99.5% (2010 est.)

School life expectancy (primary to tertiary education):
      <u>total</u>: 14 years
      <u>male</u>: 14 years
      <u>female</u>: 15 years (2008)
Unemployment, youth ages 15-24:
      <u>total</u>: 18.3%
      <u>country comparison to the world</u>: 64
      <u>male</u>: 17.7%
      <u>female</u>: 19.1% (2009)

Chapter 4: Government

Country name:

 conventional long form: Russian Federation
 conventional short form: Russia
 local long form: Rossiyskaya Federatsiya
 local short form: Rossiya
 former: Russian Empire, Russian Soviet Federative Socialist Republic

Government type:

 federation

Capital:

 name: Moscow
 geographic coordinates: 55 45 N, 37 36 E
 time difference: UTC+4 (9 hours ahead of Washington, DC during Standard Time)
 daylight saving time: +1hr; note - Russia has announced that it will remain on daylight saving time permanently, which began on 27 March 2011
 note: Russia is divided into 9 time zones

Administrative divisions:

 46 provinces (oblastey, singular - oblast), 21 republics (respublik, singular - respublika), 4 autonomous okrugs (avtonomnykh okrugov, singular - avtonomnyy okrug), 9 krays (krayev, singular - kray), 2 federal cities (goroda, singular - gorod), and 1 autonomous oblast (avtonomnaya oblast')

 oblasts: Amur (Blagoveshchensk), Arkhangel'sk, Astrakhan', Belgorod, Bryansk, Chelyabinsk, Irkutsk, Ivanovo, Kaliningrad, Kaluga, Kemerovo, Kirov, Kostroma, Kurgan, Kursk, Leningrad, Lipetsk, Magadan, Moscow, Murmansk, Nizhniy Novgorod, Novgorod, Novosibirsk, Omsk, Orenburg, Orel, Penza, Pskov, Rostov, Ryazan', Sakhalin (Yuzhno-Sakhalinsk), Samara, Saratov, Smolensk, Sverdlovsk (Yekaterinburg), Tambov, Tomsk,

Tula, Tver', Tyumen', Ul'yanovsk, Vladimir, Volgograd, Vologda, Voronezh, Yaroslavl'

republics: Adygeya (Maykop), Altay (Gorno-Altaysk), Bashkortostan (Ufa), Buryatiya (Ulan-Ude), Chechnya (Groznyy), Chuvashiya (Cheboksary), Dagestan (Makhachkala), Ingushetiya (Magas), Kabardino-Balkariya (Nal'chik), Kalmykiya (Elista), Karachayevo-Cherkesiya (Cherkessk), Kareliya (Petrozavodsk), Khakasiya (Abakan), Komi (Syktyvkar), Mariy-El (Yoshkar-Ola), Mordoviya (Saransk), North Ossetia (Vladikavkaz), Sakha [Yakutiya] (Yakutsk), Tatarstan (Kazan'), Tyva (Kyzyl), Udmurtiya (Izhevsk)

autonomous okrugs: Chukotka (Anadyr'), Khanty-Mansi (Khanty-Mansiysk), Nenets (Nar'yan-Mar), Yamalo-Nenets (Salekhard)

krays: Altay (Barnaul), Kamchatka (Petropavlovsk-Kamchatskiy), Khabarovsk, Krasnodar, Krasnoyarsk, Perm', Primorskiy [Maritime] (Vladivostok), Stavropol', Zabaykal'sk (Chita)

federal cities: Moscow [Moskva], Saint Petersburg [Sankt-Peterburg]

autonomous oblast: Yevrey [Jewish] (Birobidzhan)

note: administrative divisions have the same names as their administrative centers (exceptions have the administrative center name following in parentheses)

Independence:

24 August 1991 (from the Soviet Union); notable earlier dates: 1157 (Principality of Vladimir-Suzdal created); 16 January 1547 (Tsardom of Muscovy established); 22 October 1721 (Russian Empire proclaimed); 30 December 1922 (Soviet Union established)

National holiday:

Russia Day, 12 June (1990)

Constitution:

adopted 12 December 1993

Legal system:

civil law system; judicial review of legislative acts

International law organization participation:
has not submitted an ICJ jurisdiction declaration; non-party state to the ICCt

Suffrage:
18 years of age; universal

Executive branch:
chief of state: President Vladimir Vladimirovich PUTIN (since 7 May 2012)

head of government: Dmitriy Anatolyevich MEDVEDEV (since 8 May 2012); First Deputy Premier Igor Ivanovich SHUVALOV (since 12 May 2008); Deputy Premiers Arkadiy Vladimirovich DVORKOVICH (since 21 May 2012), Olga Yuryevna GOLODETS (since 21 May 2012), Aleksandr Gennadiyevich KHLOPONIN (since 19 January 2010), Dmitriy Nikolayevich KOZAK (since 14 October 2008), Dmitriy Olegovich ROGOZIN (since 23 December 2011), Vladislav Yuryevich SURKOV (since 27 December 2011)

cabinet: the "Government" is composed of the premier, his deputies, and ministers; all are appointed by the president, and the premier is also confirmed by the Duma

note: there is also a Presidential Administration (PA) that provides staff and policy support to the president, drafts presidential decrees, and coordinates policy among government agencies; a Security Council also reports directly to the president

elections: president elected by popular vote for a six-year term (eligible for a second term); election last held 4 March 2012 (next to be held in March 2018); note - the term length was extended from four to six years in late 2008 and went into effect after the 2012 election; there is no vice president; if the president dies in office, cannot exercise his powers because of ill health, is impeached, or resigns, the premier serves as acting president until a new presidential election is held, which must be within three months; premier appointed by the president with the approval of the Duma election results: Vladimir PUTIN elected president; percent of vote - Vladimir PUTIN 63.6%, Gennadiy ZYUGANOV 17.2%, Mikhail PROKHOROV 8%, Vladimir ZHIRINOVSKIY 6.2%, Sergey MIRONOV 3.9%, other 1.1%; Dmitriy MEDVEDEV approved by Duma 299 to 144

Legislative branch:

bicameral Federal Assembly or Federalnoye Sobraniye consists of an upper house, the Federation Council or Sovet Federatsii (166 seats; members appointed by the top executive and legislative officials in each of the 83 federal administrative units - oblasts, krays, republics, autonomous okrugs and oblasts, and the federal cities of Moscow and Saint Petersburg; members to serve four-year terms) and a lower house, the State Duma or Gosudarstvennaya Duma (450 seats; as of 2007, all members elected by proportional representation from party lists winning at least 7% of the vote; members elected by popular vote to serve four-year terms)

elections: State Duma - last held on 4 December 2011 (next to be held in December 2015)

election results: State Duma - United Russia 49.6%, CPRF 19.2%, Just Russia 13.2%, LDPR 11.7%, other 6.3%; total seats by party - United Russia 238, CPRF 92, Just Russia 64, LDPR 56

Judicial branch:

Constitutional Court; Supreme Court; Supreme Arbitration Court; judges for all courts are appointed for life by the Federation Council on the recommendation of the president

Political parties and leaders:

A Just Russia [Sergey MIRONOV]; Communist Party of the Russian Federation or CPRF [Gennadiy ZYUGANOV]; Liberal Democratic Party of Russia or LDPR [Vladimir ZHIRINOVSKIY]; Right Cause [Andrey DUNAYEV]; Rodina [Aleksey ZHURAVLEV]; United Russia [Dmitriy MEDVEDEV]; Yabloko Party [Sergey MITROKHIN]

Political pressure groups and leaders:

Association of Citizens with Initiative of Russia (TIGR); Confederation of Labor of Russia (KTR); Federation of Independent Labor Unions of Russia; Freedom of Choice Interregional Organization of Automobilists; Glasnost Defense Foundation; Golos Association in Defense of Voters' Rights; Greenpeace Russia; Human Rights Watch (Russian chapter); Institute for Collective Action; Memorial (human rights group); Movement Against Illegal Migration; Pamjat (preservation of historical monuments and recording of history); PARNAS; Russian Orthodox Church; Russian Federation of Car Owners; Russian-Chechen Friendship Society; Solidarnost; SOVA Analytical-Information Center; Union of the Committees of Soldiers' Mothers; World Wildlife Fund (Russian chapter)

International organization participation:

APEC, Arctic Council, ARF, ASEAN (dialogue partner), BIS, BRICS, BSEC, CBSS, CD, CE, CERN (observer), CICA, CIS, CSTO, EAEC, EAPC, EAS, EBRD, FAO, FATF, G-20, G-8, GCTU, IAEA, IBRD, ICAO, ICC (national committees), ICRM, IDA, IFC, IFRCS, IHO, ILO, IMF, IMO, IMSO, Interpol, IOC, IOM (observer), IPU, ISO, ITSO, ITU, ITUC (NGOs), LAIA (observer), MIGA, MINURSO, MONUSCO, NSG, OAS (observer), OIC (observer), OPCW, OSCE, Paris Club, PCA, PFP, SCO, UN, UNCTAD, UNESCO, UNHCR, UNIDO, UNISFA, UNMIL, UNMISS, UNOCI, UNSC (permanent), UNTSO, UNWTO, UPU, WCO, WFTU (NGOs), WHO, WIPO, WMO, WTO, ZC

Diplomatic representation in the US:

chief of mission: Ambassador Sergey Ivanovich KISLYAK

chancery: 2650 Wisconsin Avenue NW, Washington, DC 20007

telephone: [1] (202) 298-5700, 5701, 5704, 5708

FAX: [1] (202) 298-5735

consulate(s) general: Houston, New York, San Francisco, Seattle

Diplomatic representation from the US:

chief of mission: Ambassador Michael A. MCFAUL

embassy: Bolshoy Deviatinskiy Pereulok No. 8, 121099 Moscow

mailing address: PSC-77, APO AE 09721

telephone: [7] (495) 728-5000

FAX: [7] (495) 728-5090

consulate(s) general: Saint Petersburg, Vladivostok, Yekaterinburg

Flag description:

three equal horizontal bands of white (top), blue, and red
note: the colors may have been based on those of the Dutch flag; despite many popular interpretations, there is no official meaning assigned to the colors of the Russian flag; this flag inspired other Slav countries to adopt horizontal tricolors of the same colors but in different arrangements, and so red, blue, and white became the Pan-Slav colors

National symbol(s):

bear; double-headed eagle

National anthem:

name: "Gimn Rossiyskoy Federatsii" (National Anthem of the Russian Federation)

lyrics/music: Sergei Vladimirovich MIKHALKOV/Alexandr Vasilievich ALEXANDROV

note: in 2000, Russia adopted the tune of the anthem of the former Soviet Union (composed in 1939); the lyrics, also adopted in 2000, were written by the same person who authored the Soviet lyrics in 1943

Key Leaders

Pres.	**Vladimir Vladimirovich PUTIN**

Premier	**Dmitriy Anatolyevich MEDVEDEV**
First Dep. Premier	**Igor Ivanovich SHUVALOV**
Dep. Premier	**Arkadiy Vladimirovich DVORKOVICH**
Dep. Premier	**Olga Yuryevna GOLODETS**
Dep. Premier	**Aleksandr Gennadiyevich KHLOPONIN**
Dep. Premier	**Dmitriy Nikolayevich KOZAK**
Dep. Premier	**Dmitriy Olegovich ROGOZIN**
Dep. Premier	**Sergey Eduardovich PRIKHODKO**
Dep. Premier	**Yuriy Petrovich TRUTNEV**
Min. of Agriculture	**Nikolay Vasilyevich FEDOROV**
Min. of Civil Defense, Emergencies, & Natural Disasters	**Vladimir Andreyevich PUCHKOV**
Min. of Communications & Mass Media	**Nikolay Anatolyevich NIKIFOROV**
Min. of Culture	**Vladimir Rostislavovich MEDINSKIY**

Min. of Defense	**Sergey Kuzhugetovich SHOYGU**
Min. of Economic Development	**Aleksey Valentinovich ULYUKAYEV**
Min. of Education & Science	**Dmitriy Viktorovich LIVANOV**
Min. of Energy	**Aleksandr Valentinovich NOVAK**
Min. of Far East Development	**Akejsabdr Sergeyevich GALUSHKA**
Min. of Finance	**Anton Germanovich SILUANOV**
Min. of Foreign Affairs	**Sergey Viktorovich LAVROV**
Min. of Health	**Veronika Igoryevna SKVORTSOVA**
Min. of Industry & Trade	**Denis Valentinovich MANTUROV**
Min. of Internal Affairs	**Vladimir Aleksandrovich KOLOKOLTSEV**
Min. of Justice	**Aleksandr Vladimirovich KONOVALOV**
Min. of Labor & Social Protection	**Maksim Anatolyevich**

	TOPILIN
Min. of Natural Resources & Ecology	**Sergey Yefimovich DONSKOY**
Min. of Regional Development	**Igor Nikolayevich SLYUNYAYEV**
Min. of Sport	**Vitaliy Leontyevich MUTKO**
Min. of Transportation	**Maksim Yuryevich SOKOLOV**
Min. for Liaison With Open Govt.	**Mikhail Anatolyevich ABYZOV**
Dir., Foreign Intelligence Service (SVR)	**Mikhail Yefimovich FRADKOV**
Dir., Federal Security Service (FSB)	**Aleksandr Vasilyevich BORTNIKOV**
Sec., Security Council	**Nikolay Platonovich PATRUSHEV**
Procurator Gen.	**Yuriy Yakovlevich CHAYKA**
Chmn., Central Bank of Russia	**Elvira Sakhipzadovna NABIULLINA**
Ambassador to the US	**Sergey Ivanovich KISLYAK**
Permanent Representative to the UN, New York	**Vitaliy Ivanovich CHURKIN**

Chapter 5: Economy

Economy - overview:

Russia has undergone significant changes since the collapse of the Soviet Union, moving from a globally-isolated, centrally-planned economy to a more market-based and globally-integrated economy. Economic reforms in the 1990s privatized most industry, with notable exceptions in the energy and defense-related sectors. The protection of property rights is still weak and the private sector remains subject to heavy state interference. Russian industry is primarily split between globally-competitive commodity producers. In 2011, Russia became the world's leading oil producer, surpassing Saudi Arabia; Russia is the second-largest producer of natural gas; Russia holds the world's largest natural gas reserves, the second-largest coal reserves, and the eighth-largest crude oil reserves. Russia is also a top exporter of metals such as steel and primary aluminum. Russia's reliance on commodity exports makes it vulnerable to boom and bust cycles that follow the volatile swings in global prices. The government since 2007 has embarked on an ambitious program to reduce this dependency and build up the country's high technology sectors, but with few results so far. The economy had averaged 7% growth in the decade following the 1998 Russian financial crisis, resulting in a doubling of real disposable incomes and the emergence of a middle class. The Russian economy, however, was one of the hardest hit by the 2008-09 global economic crisis as oil prices plummeted and the foreign credits that Russian banks and firms relied on dried up. According to the World Bank the government's anti-crisis package in 2008-09 amounted to roughly 6.7% of GDP. The economic decline bottomed out in mid-2009 and the economy began to grow in the third quarter of 2009. High oil prices buoyed Russian growth in 2011-12 and helped Russia reduce the budget deficit inherited from 2008-09. Russia has reduced unemployment to a record low and has lowered inflation below double digit rates. Russia joined the World Trade Organization in 2012, which will reduce trade barriers and help open foreign markets for Russian goods. At the same time, Russia has sought to cement economic ties with countries in the former Soviet space through a Customs Union with Belarus and Kazakhstan, and, in the next several years, through a new Russia-led economic bloc called the Eurasian Union. Russia has had difficulty attracting captial and has suffered large capital outflows in the past several years, leading to official programs to improve Russia's international rankings for its investment climate. Russia's long-term challenges also include a shrinking workforce, intractable large- and small-scale corruption, and underinvestment in infrastructure.

GDP (purchasing power parity):
> $2.509 trillion (2012 est.)
> country comparison to the world: 7
> $2.422 trillion (2011 est.)
> $2.322 trillion (2010 est.)
> note: data are in 2012 US dollars

GDP (official exchange rate):
> $1.954 trillion (2012 est.)

GDP - real growth rate:
> 3.6% (2012 est.)
> country comparison to the world: 96
> 4.3% (2011)
> 4.3% (2010)

GDP - per capita (PPP):
> $17,700 (2012 est.)
> country comparison to the world: 71
> $17,000 (2011 est.)
> $16,300 (2010 est.)
> note: data are in 2012 US dollars

GDP - composition by sector:

    agriculture: 4.4%

    industry: 37.6%

    services: 58% (2012 est.)

Labor force:

    75.24 million (2012 est.)

    country comparison to the world: 8

Labor force - by occupation:

    agriculture: 9.8%

    industry: 27.5%

    services: 62.7% (2010)

Unemployment rate:

    6.2% (2012 est.)

    country comparison to the world: 62

    6.6% (2011 est.)

Population below poverty line:

    13.1% (2010)

Household income or consumption by percentage share:

    lowest 10%: 2.8%

    highest 10%: 31.7% (2009 est.)

Distribution of family income - Gini index:

    42 (2010)

    country comparison to the world: 51

    39.9 (2001)

Investment (gross fixed):

    23.2% of GDP (2012 est.)

    country comparison to the world: 60

Budget:

    revenues: $413 billion

    expenditures: $414 billion (2012 est.)

Taxes and other revenues:

    21.1% of GDP (2012 est.)

    country comparison to the world: 152

Budget surplus (+) or deficit (-):

    -0.1% of GDP (2012 est.)

    country comparison to the world: 44

Public debt:

    11% of GDP (2012 est.)

country comparison to the world: 139
8.3% of GDP (2011 est.)
note: data covers general government debt, and includes debt instruments issued (or owned) by government entities other than the treasury; the data include treasury debt held by foreign entities; the data include debt issued by subnational entities, as well as intra-governmental debt; intra-governmental debt consists of treasury borrowings from surpluses in the social funds, such as for retirement, medical care, and unemployment. Debt instruments for the social funds are not sold at public auctions.

Inflation rate (consumer prices):
5.3% (2012 est.)
country comparison to the world: 144
8.4% (2011 est.)

Central bank discount rate:
8.25% (31 December 2012 est.)
country comparison to the world: 34
8% (31 December 2011)

Commercial bank prime lending rate:
9.3% (31 December 2012 est.)
country comparison to the world: 113
8.45% (31 December 2011 est.)

Stock of narrow money:
$347 billion (31 December 2012 est.)
country comparison to the world: 15
$277.5 billion (31 December 2011 est.)

Stock of broad money:
$952.2 billion (31 December 2012 est.)
country comparison to the world: 20
$787.9 billion (31 December 2011 est.)

Stock of domestic credit:
$873.7 billion (31 December 2012 est.)
country comparison to the world: 18
$712.5 billion (31 December 2011 est.)

Market value of publicly traded shares:
$796.4 billion (31 December 2011 est.)

country comparison to the world: 17
$1.005 trillion (31 December 2010)
$861.4 billion (31 December 2009 est.)

Agriculture - products:
grain, sugar beets, sunflower seed, vegetables, fruits; beef, milk

Industrial production growth rate:
4.7% (2011 est.)
country comparison to the world: 73

Current account balance:
$85.06 billion (2012 est.)
country comparison to the world: 4
$100.3 billion (2011 est.)

Exports:
$542.5 billion (2012 est.)
country comparison to the world: 9
$520.3 billion (2011 est.)

Exports - commodities:
petroleum and petroleum products, natural gas, metals, wood and wood products, chemicals, and a wide variety of civilian and military manufactures

Exports - partners:
Netherlands 12.2%, China 6.4%, Italy 5.6%, Germany 4.6%, Poland 4.2% (2011)

Imports:
$358.1 billion (2012 est.)
country comparison to the world: 16
$322.3 billion (2011 est.)

Imports - commodities:
machinery, vehicles, pharmaceutical products, plastic, semi-finished metal products, meat, fruits and nuts, optical and medical instruments, iron, steel

Imports - partners:
China 15.5%, Germany 10%, Ukraine 6.6%, Italy 4.3% (2011)

Reserves of foreign exchange and gold:
$561.1 billion (31 December 2012 est.)

country comparison to the world: 4
$498.6 billion (31 December 2011 est.)
Debt - external:
$455.2 billion (31 December 2012 est.)
country comparison to the world: 25
$538.6 billion (31 December 2010 est.)
Stock of direct foreign investment - at home:
$596.2 billion (31 December 2012 est.)
country comparison to the world: 13
$546.2 billion (31 December 2011 est.)
Stock of direct foreign investment - abroad:
$487.4 billion (31 December 2012 est.)
country comparison to the world: 14
$436.4 billion (31 December 2011 est.)
Exchange rates:
Russian rubles (RUB) per US dollar -
31.32 (2012 est.)
29.382 (2011 est.)
30.368 (2010 est.)
31.74 (2009)
24.853 (2008)
Fiscal year:
calendar year

Chapter 6: Energy

Electricity - production:
    983.2 billion kWh (2010 est.)
    country comparison to the world: 5

Electricity - consumption:
    808 billion kWh (2009 est.)
    country comparison to the world: 6

Electricity - exports:
    19.01 billion kWh (2010 est.)
    country comparison to the world: 10

Electricity - imports:
    1.644 billion kWh (2010 est.)
    country comparison to the world: 51

Electricity - installed generating capacity:
    225.3 million kW (2009 est.)
    country comparison to the world: 5

Electricity - from fossil fuels:
    68.3% of total installed capacity (2009 est.)
    country comparison to the world: 112

Electricity - from nuclear fuels:
    10.3% of total installed capacity (2009 est.)
    country comparison to the world: 19

Electricity - from hydroelectric plants:
    20.9% of total installed capacity (2009 est.)
    country comparison to the world: 90

Electricity - from other renewable sources:
    0% of total installed capacity (2009 est.)
    country comparison to the world: 180

Crude oil - production:
    10.21 million bbl/day (2011 est.)
    country comparison to the world: 2

Crude oil - exports:
    5.43 million bbl/day (2009 est.)
    country comparison to the world: 3

Crude oil - imports:

42,000 bbl/day (2009 est.)

country comparison to the world: 60

Crude oil - proved reserves:

60 billion bbl (1 January 2012 est.)

country comparison to the world: 9

Refined petroleum products - production:

4.802 million bbl/day (2008 est.)

country comparison to the world: 5

Refined petroleum products - consumption:

3.145 million bbl/day (2011 est.)

country comparison to the world: 7

Refined petroleum products - exports:

1.924 million bbl/day (2008 est.)

country comparison to the world: 3

Refined petroleum products - imports:

21,340 bbl/day (2008 est.)

country comparison to the world: 104

Natural gas - production:

669.6 billion cu m (2011 est.)

country comparison to the world: 2

Natural gas - consumption:

506.7 billion cu m (2011 est.)

country comparison to the world: 3

Natural gas - exports:

203.9 billion cu m (2011 est.)

country comparison to the world: 2

Natural gas - imports:

41 billion cu m (2011 est.)

country comparison to the world: 11

Natural gas - proved reserves:

47.57 trillion cu m (1 January 2012 est.)

country comparison to the world: 2

Carbon dioxide emissions from consumption of energy:

1.634 billion Mt (2010 est.)

country comparison to the world: 5

Chapter 7: Communications

Telephones - main lines in use:
> 44.152 million (2011)
> country comparison to the world: 5

Telephones - mobile cellular:
> 236.7 million (2011)
> country comparison to the world: 6

Telephone system:
> general assessment: the telephone system is experiencing significant changes; there are more than 1,000 companies licensed to offer communication services; access to digital lines has improved, particularly in urban centers; Internet and e-mail services are improving; Russia has made progress toward building the telecommunications infrastructure necessary for a market economy; the estimated number of mobile subscribers jumped from fewer than 1 million in 1998 to more than 235 million in 2011; fixed line service has improved but a large demand remains
>
> domestic: cross-country digital trunk lines run from Saint Petersburg to Khabarovsk, and from Moscow to Novorossiysk; the telephone systems in 60 regional capitals have modern digital infrastructures; cellular services, both analog and digital, are available in many areas; in rural areas, the telephone services are still outdated, inadequate, and low density
>
> international: country code - 7; Russia is connected internationally by undersea fiber optic cables; satellite earth stations provide access to Intelsat, Intersputnik, Eutelsat, Inmarsat, and Orbita systems

Broadcast media:
> 6 national TV stations with the federal government owning 1 and holding a controlling interest in a second; state-owned Gazprom maintains a controlling interest in a third national channel; government-affiliated Bank Rossiya

owns controlling interest in a fourth and fifth, while the sixth national channel is owned by the Moscow city administration; roughly 3,300 national, regional, and local TV stations with over two-thirds completely or partially controlled by the federal or local governments; satellite TV services are available; 2 state-run national radio networks with a third majority-owned by Gazprom; roughly 2,400 public and commercial radio stations (2007)

Internet country code:

.ru

note - Russia also has responsibility for a legacy domain ".su" that was allocated to the Soviet Union and is being phased out

Internet hosts:

14.865 million (2012)

country comparison to the world: 10

Internet users:

40.853 million (2009)

country comparison to the world: 10

Chapter 8: Transportation

Airports:
>1,218 (2012)
>country comparison to the world: 5

Airports - with paved runways:
>total: 593
>over 3,047 m: 54
>2,438 to 3,047 m: 198
>1,524 to 2,437 m: 125
>914 to 1,523 m: 95
>under 914 m: 121 (2012)

Airports - with unpaved runways:
>total: 625
>over 3,047 m: 3
>2,438 to 3,047 m: 14
>1,524 to 2,437 m: 69
>914 to 1,523 m: 85
>under 914 m: 454 (2012)

Heliports:
>48 (2012)

Pipelines:
>condensate 122 km; gas 160,952 km; liquid petroleum gas 127 km; oil 77,630 km; oil/gas/water 38 km; refined products 13,658 km (2010)

Railways:
>total: 87,157 km
>country comparison to the world: 2
>broad gauge: 86,200 km 1.520-m gauge (40,300 km electrified)
>narrow gauge: 957 km 1.067-m gauge (on Sakhalin Island)
>note: an additional 30,000 km of non-common carrier lines serve industries (2006)

Roadways:
>total: 982,000 km
>country comparison to the world: 7

paved: 776,000 km (includes 30,000 km of expressways)

unpaved: 206,000 km

note: includes public, local, and departmental roads (2009)

Waterways:

102,000 km (including 48,000 km with guaranteed depth; the 72,000 km system in European Russia links Baltic Sea, White Sea, Caspian Sea, Sea of Azov, and Black Sea) (2009)

country comparison to the world: 2

Merchant marine:

total: 1,143

country comparison to the world: 11

by type: bulk carrier 20, cargo 642, carrier 3, chemical tanker 57, combination ore/oil 42, container 13, passenger 15, passenger/cargo 7, petroleum tanker 244, refrigerated cargo 84, roll on/roll off 13, specialized tanker 3

foreign-owned: 155 (Belgium 4, Cyprus 13, Estonia 1, Ireland 1, Italy 14, Latvia 2, Netherlands 2, Romania 1, South Korea 1, Switzerland 3, Turkey 101, Ukraine 12)

registered in other countries: 439 (Antigua and Barbuda 3, Belgium 1, Belize 30, Bulgaria 2, Cambodia 50, Comoros 12, Cook Islands 1, Cyprus 46, Dominica 3, Georgia 6, Hong Kong 1, Kiribati 1, Liberia 109, Malaysia 2, Malta 45, Marshall Islands 5, Moldova 5, Mongolia 2, Panama 49, Romania 1, Saint Kitts and Nevis 13, Saint Vincent and the Grenadines 11, Sierra Leone 7, Singapore 2, Spain 6, Vanuatu 7, unknown 19) (2010)

Ports and terminals:

Kaliningrad, Kavkaz, Nakhodka, Novorossiysk, Primorsk, Saint Petersburg, Vostochnyy

Chapter 9: Military

Military branches:

Ground Forces (Sukhoputnyye Voyskia, SV), Navy (Voyenno-Morskoy Flot, VMF), Air Forces (Voyenno-Vozdushniye Sily, VVS); Airborne Troops (Vozdushno-Desantnyye Voyska, VDV), Strategic Rocket Forces (Raketnyye Voyska Strategicheskogo Naznacheniya, RVSN), and Aerospace Defense Troops (Voyska Vozdushno-Kosmicheskoy Oborony or Voyska VKO) are independent "combat arms," not subordinate to any of the three branches; Russian Ground Forces include the following combat arms: motorized-rifle troops, tank troops, missile and artillery troops, air defense of the ground troops (2010)

Military service age and obligation:

18-27 years of age for compulsory or voluntary military service; males are registered for the draft at 17 years of age; service obligation - 1 year (conscripts can only be sent to combat zones after 6 months of training); reserve obligation to age 50

note: the chief of the General Staff Mobilization Directorate announced in March 2009 that for health reasons, only 65% of draftees in 2008 were fit for military service, and over half of these had health-induced restrictions on deployment; the deputy chief of the Russian Army General Staff confirmed in May 2011 that over 30% of potential conscripts were turned down on health grounds; 61% of draft-age Russian males receive some type of deferment each draft cycle (2011)

Manpower available for military service:

males age 16-49: 34,132,156

females age 16-49: 34,985,115 (2010 est.)

Manpower fit for military service:

males age 16-49: 20,431,035

females age 16-49: 26,381,518 (2010 est.)

Manpower reaching militarily significant age annually:

    <u>male</u>: 693,843

    <u>female</u>: 660,359 (2010 est.)

Military expenditures:

    3.9% of GDP (2005)

    <u>country comparison to the world</u>: 25

Chapter 10: Transnational Issues

Disputes - international:

Russia remains concerned about the smuggling of poppy derivatives from Afghanistan through Central Asian countries; China and Russia have demarcated the once disputed islands at the Amur and Ussuri confluence and in the Argun River in accordance with the 2004 Agreement, ending their centuries-long border disputes; the sovereignty dispute over the islands of Etorofu, Kunashiri, Shikotan, and the Habomai group, known in Japan as the "Northern Territories" and in Russia as the "Southern Kurils," occupied by the Soviet Union in 1945, now administered by Russia, and claimed by Japan, remains the primary sticking point to signing a peace treaty formally ending World War II hostilities; Russia's military support and subsequent recognition of Abkhazia and South Ossetia independence in 2008 continue to sour relations with Georgia; Azerbaijan, Kazakhstan, and Russia ratified Caspian seabed delimitation treaties based on equidistance, while Iran continues to insist on a one-fifth slice of the sea; Norway and Russia signed a comprehensive maritime boundary agreement in 2010; various groups in Finland advocate restoration of Karelia (Kareliya) and other areas ceded to the Soviet Union following World War II but the Finnish Government asserts no territorial demands; Russia and Estonia signed a technical border agreement in May 2005, but Russia recalled its signature in June 2005 after the Estonian parliament added to its domestic ratification act a historical preamble referencing the Soviet occupation and Estonia's pre-war borders under the 1920 Treaty of Tartu; Russia contends that the preamble allows Estonia to make territorial claims on Russia in the future, while Estonian officials deny that the preamble has any legal impact on the treaty text; Russia demands better treatment of the Russian-speaking population in Estonia and Latvia;

Lithuania and Russia committed to demarcating their boundary in 2006 in accordance with the land and maritime treaty ratified by Russia in May 2003 and by Lithuania in 1999; Lithuania operates a simplified transit regime for Russian nationals traveling from the Kaliningrad coastal exclave into Russia, while still conforming, as an EU member state with an EU external border, where strict Schengen border rules apply; preparations for the demarcation delimitation of land boundary with Ukraine have commenced; the dispute over the boundary between Russia and Ukraine through the Kerch Strait and Sea of Azov remains unresolved despite a December 2003 framework agreement and on-going expert-level discussions; Kazakhstan and Russia boundary delimitation was ratified on November 2005 and field demarcation should commence in 2007; Russian Duma has not yet ratified 1990 Bering Sea Maritime Boundary Agreement with the US; Denmark (Greenland) and Norway have made submissions to the Commission on the Limits of the Continental shelf (CLCS) and Russia is collecting additional data to augment its 2001 CLCS submission

Refugees and internally displaced persons:

IDPs: 8,500-28,450 (displacement from Chechnya and North Ossetia-Alania) (2011)

Trafficking in persons:

current situation: Russia is a source, transit, and destination country for men, women, and children trafficked for various purposes; people from Russia and other countries, including Belarus, Tajikistan, and Uzbekistan, are subjected to conditions of forced labor in Russia; children are subjected to prostitution in large Russian cities and to forced begging; Russian women were reported to be victims of sex trafficking in many countries, including in Northeast Asia, Europe, and throughout the Middle East tier rating: Tier 2 Watch List - Russia failed to show evidence of increased efforts to combat trafficking; victim protection in Russia remains very weak, as the government allocated scant funding for victim shelters and little funding for anti-trafficking efforts by governmental or non-governmental organizations; the government did not make discernible efforts to fund a national awareness campaign, although some local efforts were assisted by local government funding (2008)

Illicit drugs:

limited cultivation of illicit cannabis and opium poppy and producer of methamphetamine, mostly for domestic consumption; government has active illicit crop eradication program; used as transshipment point for Asian opiates, cannabis, and Latin American cocaine bound for growing domestic markets, to a lesser extent Western and Central Europe, and occasionally to the US; major source of heroin precursor chemicals; corruption and organized crime are key concerns; major consumer of opiates

Other Key Facts™ Titles

All Key Facts™ Titles are Available at

www.Amazon.com

THE INTERNATIONALIST®

2013

WWW.INTERNATIONALIST.COM

www.ingramcontent.com/pod-product-compliance
Lightning Source LLC
Chambersburg PA
CBHW051302170526
45165CB00004B/1817